Daily Math Practice　　　# Monday

1. 7 – 5 = _____

2.　3
　　+ 6

3. Make an **X** on the second ball.

4. Write the number.

eight ____　　　four ____

two ____

5. There were three red fish, two blue fish, and five yellow fish. How many fish in all?

_____ fish

Daily Math Practice　　　# Tuesday ⟨ 1 ⟩

1. 9 – 3 = _____

2.　7
　　+ 3

3.

= _____ ¢

4. How many?

 _____

5. At a party, 9 friends ate cake and 6 friends ate cookies. How many more ate cake than cookies?

_____ more ate cake

1. $9 - 9 =$ _____

2. $\begin{array}{r} 5 \\ + 3 \\ \hline \end{array}$

3. Mark the triangles.

4. What time is it?

_____

5. Eric had a dime. He spent 6¢. How much change did he get back?

_____¢

---

1. $8 - 2 =$ _____

2. $\begin{array}{r} 2 \\ + 7 \\ \hline \end{array}$

3. Mark the pair that go together.

4. Fill in the missing numbers.

___ 20 ___ ___ 50

5. Rachel has three bears, two tigers, and a giraffe. How many toy animals does she have?

_____ toy animals

EMC 6712 • © Evan-Moor Corp.

Friday ⟨1⟩

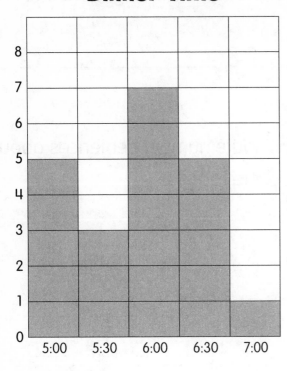

Dinner Time

1. How many people ate at these times?

7:00 _____ 5:30 _____ 6:00 _____

2. How many more people ate at 6:00 than at 7:00?

_____

3. Color a box on the graph to show the time you eat dinner.

Daily Progress Record ⟨1⟩

How many did you get correct each day? Color the squares.

	Monday	Tuesday	Wednesday	Thursday	Friday
5					
4					
3					
2					
1					

1. 7 – 0 = _____

2. 5
   +5

3.

= _____¢

4. Fill in the missing numbers.

28 ___ ___ ___ 32

5. Write number sentences about the rabbits.

____ + ____ = ____

____ – ____ = ____

1. 10 – 1 = _____

2. 8
   +2

3. How many fingers do you see?

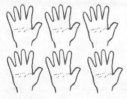

_____ fingers

4. seven

○ 6   ○ 7   ○ 17

5. Amy and Sam walk home after school. It is 5 blocks to Amy's house. Sam walks 4 more blocks. How far is it to Sam's house from school?

_____ blocks

Wednesday ⟨2⟩

1. 1 + 8 = _____

2. 10
       − 5
       ‾‾‾

3. Estimate.

   ○ 20   ○ 100   ○ 300

4. Mark the name of the shape.

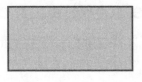

square   triangle   rectangle

5. Pierre picked 5 apples. He needs 9 apples. How many more does Pierre need to pick?

_____ apples

Thursday ⟨2⟩

1. 9 − 8 = _____

2. 6
       + 4
       ‾‾‾

3. What time is it?

____ : ____

4. What comes next?

X O X O ___ ___

5. Jan saw 9 horses run across a field. There were 5 horses that had riders. How many did not?

_____ horses

Friday ⟨2⟩

Steve went to the store for his mother. He bought bread for $1, butter for $2, eggs for $1, and milk for $3. How much did he spend?

$_____

He gave the clerk $10. How much change did he get back?

$_____

Daily Progress Record ⟨2⟩

How many did you get correct each day? Color the squares.

	Monday	Tuesday	Wednesday	Thursday	Friday
5					▓
4					▓
3					▓
2					
1					

1. 6 + 3 = _____

2.   8
      – 4

3. Make an **X** on the fifth flower.

4. Fill in the missing sign.

4 ☐ 6 = 10

5. Nicole has 5 nickels in her pocket. She has 3 nickels in the bank. How much money does Nicole have?

_____ cents

1. 6 + 4 = _____

2.   7
      – 3

3. What comes next?

32 ___   57   ___

99 ___

4. Mark the half.

5. Kurt saw 11 fireflies in the backyard, and then 6 flew away. How many are still in the backyard?

_____ fireflies

Wednesday ⬡ 3

1. $9 + 0 =$ _____

2.
$$\begin{array}{r} 8 \\ -\ 7 \\ \hline \end{array}$$

3. How far is it around the box?

3
3 ⬛ 3
3

_____

4. Which side weighs more?

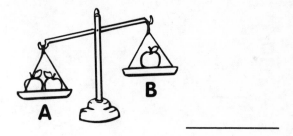

A   B

_____

5. Kai took six jelly beans. If he ate half, how many did he eat?

_____ jelly beans

Thursday ⬡ 3

1. $6 - 6 =$ _____

2.
$$\begin{array}{r} 7 \\ +\ 2 \\ \hline \end{array}$$

3. Write the number.

_____ marbles

4. Count by tens.

60 ___ ___ ___ ___

5. Mother gave Tanisha 1 dime and 10 pennies. How many 10¢ cookies can Tanisha buy?

_____ cookies

Friday ⟨3⟩

Write four number sentences about the birds.

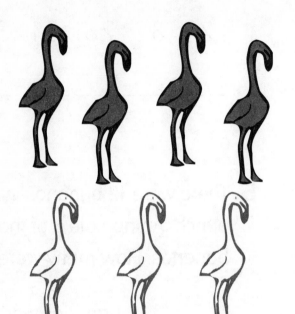

_____ + _____ = _____

_____ + _____ = _____

_____ − _____ = _____

_____ − _____ = _____

Daily Progress Record ⟨3⟩

How many did you get correct each day? Color the squares.

	Monday	Tuesday	Wednesday	Thursday	Friday
5					
4					
3					
2					
1					

1. 8 + 3 = _____

2. 10
      − 4
      ——

3. Color $\frac{1}{3}$.

4. Write the numbers in order.

29 32 28 31 30

___ ___ ___ ___ ___

5. There were 12 bananas in a bunch. An ape ate 6 of the bananas. How many were left?

_____ bananas were left

Daily Math Practice **Tuesday** 4

1. 5 − 4 = _____

2.   9
      + 2
      ——

3. What comes next if you count by tens?

20 ___ 60 ___ 90 ___

4. Fill in the missing number.

12 − = 4

5. Tammy put one sandwich, two cookies, and three carrot sticks into her lunch bag. How many things did she pack?

_____ things

1. 4 + 5 + 1 = _____

2. 7
     - 4
    ___

3. Fill in the correct symbol.

< = >

27 ◯ 41

4. Count the money.

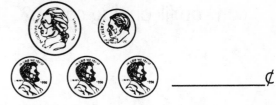 _____¢

5. There were 12 horses to feed. Father fed 5 horses. How many did Mark feed?

_____ horses

Daily Math Practice **Thursday** 4

1. 9 - 7 = _____

2. 8
     + 4
    ___

3. Name the shape.

◯ triangle   ◯ square   ◯ circle

4. Circle the odd number.

6   8   5

5. Sasha made a mark for each point he scored in the game. Look at the marks. How many points did he score?

_____ points

Friday ⟨4⟩

If you have this many eggs,
can you fill an egg carton?

$$6 - 1 + 4 - 3 + 5 + 1 = \underline{\hspace{2cm}}$$

yes   no

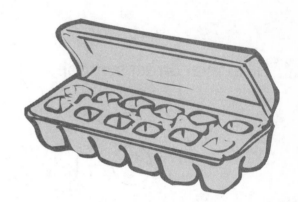

Daily Progress Record ⟨4⟩

How many did you get correct each day? Color the squares.

	Monday	Tuesday	Wednesday	Thursday	Friday
5					▓
4					▓
3					▓
2					
1					

1. $11 - 8 =$ _____

2. $\begin{array}{r} 7 \\ + 5 \\ \hline \end{array}$

3. Fill in the correct symbol.

$$< \ = \ >$$

64 ◯ 48

4. Circle the even number.

9   6   3

5. Write a word problem for $6 + 3$.

_____

_____

_____

1. $12 - 6 =$ _____

2. $\begin{array}{r} 3 \\ + 9 \\ \hline \end{array}$

3. Count by twos.

20 22 ___ ___ 28 ___

4. Mark the squares.

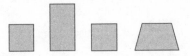

5. The balloon man at the fair had 2 orange, 5 red, 1 green, 1 blue, and 4 purple balloons. How many balloons did he have to sell?

_____ balloons

Wednesday 5

1. 5 + 6 = _____

2. 11
   − 6
   ‾‾‾‾

3. Are the two sides the same?

yes   no

4. Fill in the missing numbers.

99 ___ ___ ___ 103

5. Mother gave Brad 8 cookies. He ate 3 and gave 3 to his best friend. How many did he have left?

14   5   2

Thursday 5

1. 10 + 1 = _____

2. 12
   − 8
   ‾‾‾‾

3. 2 tens and 3 ones = _____

4. How long is the worm?

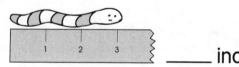

_____ inches

5. There were 12 apples on the tree, and then 7 fell off. How many were left?

_____ apples

Friday ⬡ 5

Mr. Paul asked 12 students in his class, "Do you like apples, oranges, bananas, or grapes best?" He got these answers:

apples   ////

oranges   ///

bananas   ///

grapes   //

Fill in the graph.

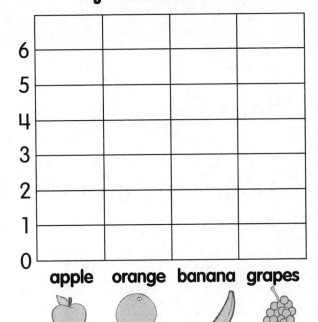

My Favorite Fruit

apple   orange   banana   grapes

Daily Progress Record ⬡ 5

How many did you get correct each day? Color the squares.

	Monday	Tuesday	Wednesday	Thursday	Friday
5					
4					
3					
2					
1					

1. $2 + 9 =$ _____

2. $\begin{array}{r} 12 \\ -\ 4 \\ \hline \end{array}$

3. Mark the shapes with 4 sides and 4 corners.

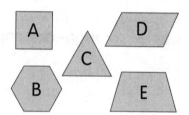

4. Count by tens.

100 110 ____ ____

5. The cook put four carrots and seven potatoes into the soup. How many vegetables were in the soup?

_____ vegetables

1. $10 - 0 =$ _____

2. $\begin{array}{r} 4 \\ +\ 7 \\ \hline \end{array}$

3. Color $\frac{1}{2}$.

4. $6 + 6 = 12$,

so $12 - 6 = $

5. Write a word problem about this number sentence.

$5 - 3 = 2$

_____

_____

_____

1. $12 - 3 =$ _____

2.
$$\begin{array}{r} 6 \\ + 6 \\ \hline \end{array}$$

3. Write the number word.

10 _____

16 _____

4. What time is it?

_____ o'clock

5. Sofia picked 9 apples, and 3 were red and 2 were green. The rest were yellow. How many apples were yellow?

_____ yellow apples

1. $11 - 2 =$ _____

2.
$$\begin{array}{r} 9 \\ + 3 \\ \hline \end{array}$$

3. Mark the names for 10.

8 + 1   5 + 5   3 + 7

6 + 4   3 + 6   8 + 2

4. Which is heavier?

5. Julio and Tony made 12 baskets altogether. If Julio made 7 of the baskets, how many did Tony make?

_____ baskets

Friday ⬡ 6

Mrs. Baker, the school cook, needs
16 loaves of bread. She bought
7 loaves at the bakery. She baked
6 loaves. How many more loaves
does she need?

_____ more loaves

Daily Progress Record ⬡ 6

How many did you get correct each day? Color the squares.

	Monday	Tuesday	Wednesday	Thursday	Friday
5					
4					
3					
2					
1					

1. 8 + 7 = _____

2. 14
   − 6
   ‾‾‾

3. Make an **X** on the sixth ant.

🐜 🐜 🐜 🐜 🐜 🐜 🐜 🐜 🐜

4. 12 > 21

      yes   no

5. Shawn went to the park at 2:00. She came home at 4:00. How long was she gone?

_____ hours

---

1. 4 + 8 + 3 = _____

2. 15
   − 9
   ‾‾‾

3. What comes next?

32 ___   57 ___

79 ___

4. 20 18 ___ ___ ___ 10

5. Peter's cat had 6 kittens. He can keep 2 kittens. His grandmother wants 1 kitten. How many kittens still need homes?

_____ kittens

1. $13 - 5 - 2 = $ _____

2. $\begin{array}{r} 4 \\ + 9 \\ \hline \end{array}$

3. 3 tens and 4 ones = _____

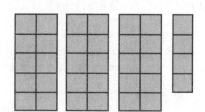

4. Color an ABCABC pattern.

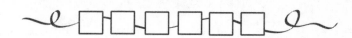

5. Kelsey had three blue ribbons, seven green ribbons, and four red ribbons. How many ribbons did she have?

_____ ribbons

1. $12 - 3 = $ _____

2. $\begin{array}{r} 12 \\ + 3 \\ \hline \end{array}$

3. Mark the one that holds the most.

○ pint   ○ gallon   ○ quart

4. $7 \boxed{} 5 = 12$

5. There were 16 stairs. Carlos walked halfway up. How many steps did he climb?

_____ steps

Friday ⟨7⟩

Complete this chart.

How many ways can you make 10?

3 1 1 9 8 2
2 4 8 4 1 5
5 5 2 6 1 1
5 7 2 1 3 9
4 1 6 2 2 0

Daily Progress Record ⟨7⟩

How many did you get correct each day? Color the squares.

	Monday	Tuesday	Wednesday	Thursday	Friday
5					
4					
3					
2					
1					

1. 15 – 6 = _____

2.
```
   3
   1
 + 8
 ___
```

3.

= _____ ¢

4. 6 + ☐ = 12

5. Write a word problem for
9 – 5 = 4.

_____

_____

_____

1. 10 – 10 = _____

2.
```
 14
 +0
 ___
```

3. Mark the things that have the same shape.

4. Write the number.

eleven ____   twelve ____

twenty ____

5. My sister likes chickens. She has eight now. How many will she have if I give her six more for her birthday?

_____ chickens

Wednesday ⟨8⟩

1. $8 + 7 =$ _____

2. $\begin{array}{r} 14 \\ -\ 5 \\ \hline \end{array}$

3. How long is the pencil?

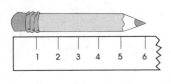

_____ cm

4. five + seven =

○ 11   ○ 12   ○ 13

5. A group of 8 girls and 5 boys went on a hike. How many went hiking? Mark the number sentence for this problem.

○ 8 – 5 =   ○ 8 + 5 =
○ 1 + 8 + 5 =

Thursday ⟨8⟩

1. $7 + 7 - 4 =$ _____

2. $\begin{array}{r} 12 \\ -\ 8 \\ \hline \end{array}$

3. Are both sides the same?

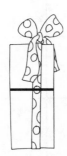

yes   no

4. $6 + 3 = 5 + 4$

yes   no

5. Alonzo wants to see a movie. He has $5. If his ticket costs $4, how much change will he get back?

$_____

Friday 8

Stu has 3 ▢s, 6 △s, and 3 ◯s.

Draw a pattern using all of his shapes.

Daily Progress Record 8

How many did you get correct each day? Color the squares.

	Monday	Tuesday	Wednesday	Thursday	Friday
5					
4					
3					
2					
1					

24

EMC 6712 • © Evan-Moor Corp.

1. $7 + 8 =$ _____

2. 13
    − 4
    ____

3. How much is it?

_____ ¢

4. 100 99 98 ___ ___

___ ___ ___ ___ ___

5. There are two mittens in a pair. How many mittens are in seven pairs?

_____ mittens

1. $13 - 9 =$ _____

2. 9
    + 4
    ____

3. About how many jelly beans are in $\frac{1}{2}$ cup?

○ 200   ○ 20   ○ 2

4. $12 + 4 = \boxed{} + 12$

5. Write number sentences using 8, 7, and 15.

___ + ___ = ___

___ + ___ = ___

___ − ___ = ___

___ − ___ = ___

Wednesday ⟨9⟩

1. $14 - 5 = \underline{\hspace{2cm}}$

2.
$$\begin{array}{r} 10 \\ + 10 \\ \hline \end{array}$$

3. Name the pattern.

_____

4. Mark the even numbers.

1 2 3 4 5 6

5. If Walter eats $\frac{1}{2}$ of his candy bar for lunch and $\frac{1}{2}$ of his candy bar for a snack after school, how much is left?

_____ is left

Thursday ⟨9⟩

1. $8 + 7 = \underline{\hspace{2cm}}$

2.
$$\begin{array}{r} 13 \\ - 6 \\ \hline \end{array}$$

3. How far is it around this shape?

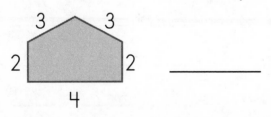 _____

4. $6 + 2 = \underline{\hspace{2cm}}$

$60 + 20 = \underline{\hspace{2cm}}$

5. Bananas cost 30¢ each. Can Luis buy two bananas if he has 4 dimes, 3 nickels, and 5 pennies?

yes   no

Friday ⟨9⟩

Color It ✎

Show nine different ways to color the balloons. Use only red, blue, and yellow crayons. Each balloon may be only **one** color.

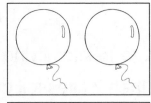 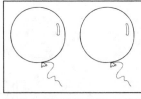 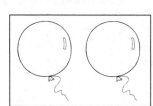

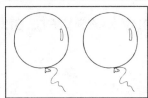 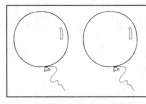 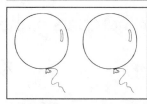

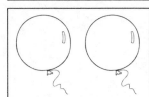 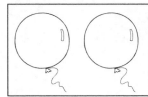 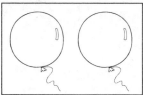

Daily Progress Record ⟨9⟩

How many did you get correct each day? Color the squares.

	Monday	Tuesday	Wednesday	Thursday	Friday
5					
4					
3					
2					
1					

Monday ⟨10⟩

1. $6 + 5 - 2 =$ _____

2.
$$\begin{array}{r} 9 \\ + 6 \\ \hline \end{array}$$

3. Mark members of the 12 family.

$6 + 6$ $8 + 2$

$3 + 9$ $5 + 7$

4. 8 is an odd number.

yes   no

5. There were 15 kites flying in the air, and then 7 kites fell down. How many kites were still in the air?

○ 22   ○ 12   ○ 8

Tuesday ⟨10⟩

1. $13 - 4 =$ _____

2.
$$\begin{array}{r} 3 \\ + 9 \\ \hline \end{array}$$

3. What time is it?

half past _____

4. $7 + 9 = 9 + 7$

yes   no

5. The zoo has 14 elephants and 6 giraffes. How many more elephants than giraffes are there?

_____ more elephants

1. $100 - 0 =$ _____

2.
$$\begin{array}{r} 5 \\ 6 \\ +\ 3 \\ \hline \end{array}$$

3. Start at the star. Where is the heart?

2			
1			
★	1	2	3

over _____ up _____

4. Mark the circle that shows $\frac{1}{4}$ shaded.

5. Each backpack has three books in it. How many books are in five backpacks?

_____ books

1. zero + eight + four = _____

2.
$$\begin{array}{r} 15 \\ -\ 6 \\ \hline \end{array}$$

3. How much does the cat weigh?

_____ pounds

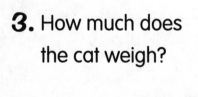

4. 4 tens and 7 ones = _____

5. David played for 5 hours today. If he played for 3 hours before lunch, how many hours did he play after lunch?

○ $5 + 3 = 8$ ○ $8 - 3 = 5$

○ $5 - 3 = 2$

Solve the problem.

two + three – four + nine – five + seven = _____

Write a problem using number words.

_____ + _____ – _____ = _____

Daily Math Practice

Daily Progress Record 〈10〉

How many did you get correct each day? Color the squares.

	Monday	Tuesday	Wednesday	Thursday	Friday
5					
4					
3					
2					
1					

EMC 6712 • © Evan-Moor Corp.

1. sixteen – nine = _____

2. 3 + 3 + 3 = _____

3.

= _____¢

4. Fill in the correct symbol.

< = >

6 + 7 ◯ 7 + 6

5. Lou sold seventeen boxes of cookies. Dawn sold fifteen boxes. How many more boxes of cookies did Lou sell?

_____ boxes of cookies

---

1. 7 ☐ 7 = 14

2.
```
   7
   3
 + 7
 ───
```

3. Write the numbers in order.

60 40 80 50 70

____ ____ ____ ____ ____

4. Write the number thirteen.

_____

5. Ted and Ann went berry picking. They picked 14 cans of berries. On the way home they ate 3 cans of berries. How many cans were left?

_____ cans

1. $9 + 8 =$ _____

2. $\begin{array}{r} 16 \\ -\ 7 \\ \hline \end{array}$

3. Count by twos.

4 ___ 10 ___

18 ___ 16 ___

4. $15 \boxed{} 8 = 7$

5. A block has 4 corners. The 4 sides are the same size. What shape is the block?

○ circle

○ square

○ rectangle

1. $12 - 5 - 3 =$ _____

2. ___ + ___ = 14

3. Draw the shape that has 3 corners and 3 sides.

4. $9 + 5 = 14$, so

$14 - 5 = \boxed{}$

5. What number is three more than $12 - 5$?

○ 10   ○ 7   ○ 17

Patty lives five blocks from school.
She rides her bike to school and back.
How many blocks does she ride in
one day?

_____ blocks in one day

How many blocks does she ride in
five days?

_____ blocks in five days

Daily Math Practice

Daily Progress Record ⬡11⬡

How many did you get correct each day? Color the squares.

	Monday	Tuesday	Wednesday	Thursday	Friday
5					▓
4					▓
3					▓
2					
1					

1. fifteen – five = _____

2. $8 + 2 + 4 =$ _____

3. Write four ways to make 14.

_____

_____

_____

_____

4.

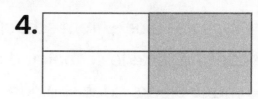

$\frac{1}{4}$ $\frac{2}{3}$ $\frac{2}{4}$

5. A group of 2 adults, 5 boys, and 6 girls went on a picnic. How many people went on the picnic?

_____ people

1. $9 + 2 =$ _____

2. $\begin{array}{r} 11 \\ -\ 6 \\ \hline \end{array}$

3. Show 2:00 on the clock.

4. 98 ____ ____ ____

____ 103

5. It took Hallie 16 minutes to eat her lunch. It took her sister 9 minutes. How much more time did Hallie take?

_____ minutes

Wednesday ⟨12⟩

1. 10 − 5 = _____

2.
$$
\begin{array}{r}
7 \\
4 \\
+\ 5 \\
\hline
\end{array}
$$

3. Mark the things that go together.

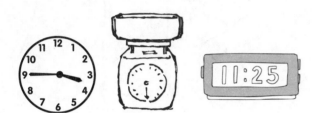

4. Fill in the correct symbol.

< = >

46 ◯ 48

5. There were 16 fish in the pond. If Cindy caught 9, how many were left?

_____ fish

Thursday ⟨12⟩

1. 2 + 1 + 9 = _____

2.
$$
\begin{array}{r}
16 \\
-\ 6 \\
\hline
\end{array}
$$

3. Mark the hexagon.

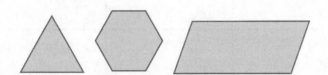

4. Count by fives.

___ 45 ___

5. It takes one dozen eggs to bake an angel food cake. Mother has four eggs. How many more does she need?

_____ more eggs

Oscar thinks the answer to this problem is 13.
Kim thinks it is 9. Mike thinks it is 12. Find the answer.

$$12 - 4 + 5 - 6 + 0 + 7 - 1 = \underline{\hspace{2cm}}$$

Who was right?

Oscar   Kim   Mike

Daily Math Practice

Daily Progress Record ⬡ 12

How many did you get correct each day? Color the squares.

	Monday	Tuesday	Wednesday	Thursday	Friday
5					▨
4					▨
3					▨
2					
1					

1. twelve + four = _____

4. $9 + 7 = 7 +$

2.
$$\begin{array}{r} 14 \\ -\ 5 \\ \hline \end{array}$$

3.

= _____ ¢

5. Jim saw 8 sea lions yesterday and 7 today. How many sea lions did Jim see?

_____ sea lions

---

1. $12 - 12 =$ _____

4. Mark the odd numbers.

1 2 3 4 5 6 7 8 9

2.
$$\begin{array}{r} 13 \\ -\ 7 \\ \hline \end{array}$$

3. Mark the cone.

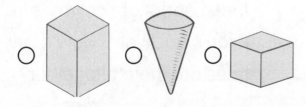

5. There were 15 pigeons on the roof. If 8 flew away, how many were left?

_____ pigeons

1. $17 - 0 =$ _____

2. $\begin{array}{r} 12 \\ +14 \\ \hline \end{array}$

3. Draw a line to make two sides that are the same.

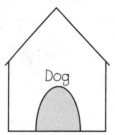

4. 108 _____ _____

_____ 112

5. How far will Alana travel if she walks six miles today and nine miles tomorrow?

_____ miles

---

1. $7 + 6 + 2 =$ _____

2. $\begin{array}{r} 28 \\ -11 \\ \hline \end{array}$

3. About how many pennies will this jar hold?

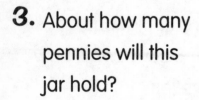

a. 500 b. 25 c. 150

4. Circle the object that is the same size and shape.

5. There are 4 apple trees, 7 pear trees, and 4 apricot trees in Ryan's backyard. How many fruit trees are there altogether?

_____ trees

Friday ⬡13

Elephants

	1 🐘	2 🐘	5 🐘
trunk	1		
ears	2		
feet	4		
tail	1		

Daily Progress Record ⬡13

How many did you get correct each day? Color the squares.

	Monday	Tuesday	Wednesday	Thursday	Friday
5					▓
4					▓
3					▓
2					▓
1					

1. $5 + 8 - 6 =$ _____

2. $17 - 7 =$ _____

3. How many feet around the pool?

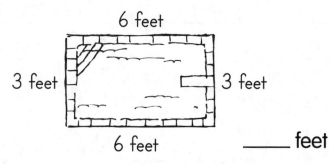

6 feet

3 feet   3 feet

6 feet   _____ feet

4. $11 \boxed{} 2 = 13$

5. Recess is 15 minutes long. Ben and Tara have been playing for 8 minutes. How much longer can they play?

_____ minutes

1. $16 - 7 =$ _____

2. $\begin{array}{r} 32 \\ + 5 \\ \hline \end{array}$

3. Make an **X** on the fourth slipper.

4. $12 + 4 = 16$, so

$16 - 4 = \boxed{}$

5. Grandma planted 4 rows of squash, 2 rows of beans, and 7 rows of corn in her garden. How many rows did she plant?

_____ rows

Wednesday ⟨14⟩

1. $9 + 3 + 5 =$ _____

2. $11 - 7 =$ _____

3.

= _____

4. Name the pattern.

_____

5. The petting zoo had 6 goats, 2 sheep, 1 pony, and 1 calf. How many animals were in the petting zoo?

_____ animals

Thursday ⟨14⟩

1. $15 - 8 - 7 =$ _____

2. $\begin{array}{r} 10 \\ + \ 2 \\ \hline \end{array}$

3. Write the time.

half past _____

4. Fill in the correct symbol.

$< \ = \ >$

$4 + 5 \bigcirc 6 - 2$

5. Emma picked twelve flowers. She put ten in a vase. How many flowers were left?

_____ flowers

Jill has three pairs of shoes. Jay has three pairs, too. How many shoes do they have in all?

_____ shoes

How many did you get correct each day? Color the squares.

	Monday	Tuesday	Wednesday	Thursday	Friday
5					
4					
3					
2					
1					

EMC 6712 • © Evan-Moor Corp.

Monday ⟨15⟩

1. $9 + 7 =$ _____

2. $\begin{array}{r} 29 \\ -\ 17 \\ \hline \end{array}$

3. Mark number nineteen.

9   29   19

4. Look at the clocks. How many minutes have passed?

2:00 ➡ 2:15

_____ minutes

5. Ronnie gathered 9 white eggs and 6 brown eggs. How many eggs did she have?

_____ eggs

Tuesday ⟨15⟩

1. $19 - 5 =$ _____

2. $\begin{array}{r} 8 \\ 3 \\ +\ 4 \\ \hline \end{array}$

3. $6 + 5 = 11$, so

$5 + 6 =$ ☐

4. 7 is an even number.

yes   no

5. Write a word problem for
$15 - 8 = 7.$

_____

_____

_____

Wednesday ⟨15⟩

1. $13 - 6 =$ _____

2. $\begin{array}{r} 43 \\ + \ 6 \\ \hline \end{array}$

3. Count by ones.

110 _____ _____ _____

4. Use tally marks to show 29.

5. Ali went to the zoo on his birthday. He asked 14 friends to go with him. If 3 couldn't go, how many friends went with him?

_____ friends

Thursday ⟨15⟩

1. $10 + 0 =$ _____

2. $\begin{array}{r} 10 \\ - \ 0 \\ \hline \end{array}$

3. Count by tens.

____ 30   ____ 60

____ 100

4. fifteen – seven – two =

_____

5. Eleven ants were on the picnic basket. If six more came, how many ants were on the basket?

○ $7 + 6 = 13$

○ $11 - 6 = 5$

○ $11 + 6 = 17$

EMC 6712 • © Evan-Moor Corp.

Friday ⟨15⟩

Make each line add up to 6.

Magic Square

across →
down ↓
corner to corner ↘

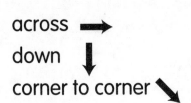

4		**0**
	2	

Daily Progress Record ⟨15⟩

How many did you get correct each day? Color the squares.

	Monday	Tuesday	Wednesday	Thursday	Friday
5					▓
4					▓
3					▓
2					▓
1					

1. 5 + 6 + 3 = _____

2. 14
   − 5

3. Circle the tool that you would use to weigh the rabbit:

4. Write eighteen.

_____

5. Annie saw 9 yellow and black moths and 6 white moths. How many moths did she see?

_____ moths

---

1. 13 − 6 = _____

2. 21
   + 18

3. Color $\frac{1}{3}$.

4. Fill in the correct symbol.

< = >

96 ◯ 69

5. Serena collected 18 rocks and shells. If she has 7 rocks, how many shells does she have?

_____ shells

Wedenesday 〈16〉

1. $15 - 8 = $ _____

2. $\begin{array}{r} 6 \\ + 7 \\ \hline \end{array}$

3. What time is it?

$4{:}45$

a quarter to _____

4. 9 is odd.

yes   no

5. Write a word problem for

$16 - 7 = 9.$

_____

_____

_____

Thursday 〈16〉

1. thirteen – seven = _____

2. $7 + 7 = $ _____

3. $9 + 8 = 17$, so

$17 - 9 = \boxed{}$

4. $11 - \boxed{} = 5$

5. Kelly has a dozen stickers. If she gives the stickers to six of her friends, how many will each friend get?

_____ stickers

Friday 〈16〉

Nadia and Bo picked vegetables from the garden. They filled 2 baskets with vegetables. Each basket had 5 ears of corn, 4 tomatoes, and 3 squash.

How many vegetables were in one basket?

_____ vegetables

How many vegetables were in two baskets?

_____ vegetables

Daily Progress Record 〈16〉

How many did you get correct each day? Color the squares.

	Monday	Tuesday	Wednesday	Thursday	Friday
5					
4					
3					
2					
1					

1. 7 + 8 = _____

2. 10
     − 3
    ____

3. Make an **X** on the seventh balloon.

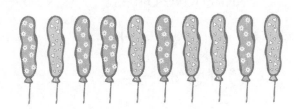

4. How much?

⁄⁄⁄⁄ ⁄⁄⁄⁄ ⁄⁄⁄⁄ ⁄

_____

5. Milton has two brothers and four sisters. How many children are in Milton's family?

_____ children

1. 30 + 9 = _____

2. 16
     − 7
    ____

3.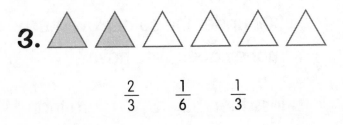

$\frac{2}{3}$ $\frac{1}{6}$ $\frac{1}{3}$

4.

a. 55¢ b. 45¢ c. 50¢

5. Mely had 15 cents. Her mother gave her 10 cents. Can she buy an ice-cream cone that costs 30 cents?

yes   no

Wednesday ⟨17⟩

1. 8 + 9 = _____

2. 25
     − 3
     ____

3. What comes before?

____97   ____100

____131   ____160

4. twenty − fourteen = _____

5. There are 15 kids on my block that have blue bikes and 4 kids that have red bikes. How many kids have bikes?

○ 1 + 5 + 4 =

○ 15 + 4 =

○ 15 − 4 =

Thursday ⟨17⟩

1. 24 + 2 = _____

2. 14
     − 9
     ____

3. Mark the cube.

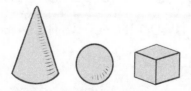

4. Count by fives.

____ ____ 15 ____ ____ 30

5. Wes has 30¢ in his bank. He has 20¢ in his pocket. He found 30¢ under the sofa. How much money does Wes have?

less than $1 $1   more than $1

EMC 6712 • © Evan-Moor Corp.

Friday ⟨17⟩

Which Toy Do You Like Best?

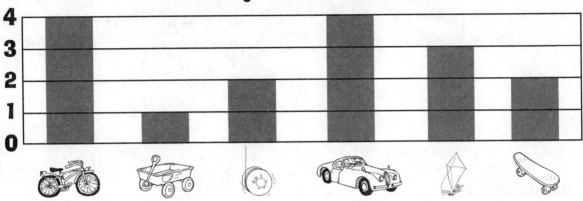

Look at the graph. What does it tell you?

I can tell:

1. _____

2. _____

Daily Progress Record ⟨17⟩

How many did you get correct each day? Color the squares.

	Monday	Tuesday	Wednesday	Thursday	Friday
5					▓
4					▓
3					▓
2					
1					

Monday ⟨18⟩

1. $8 + 8 =$ _____

2. 67
      – 5
    ‾‾‾‾

3. What time is it?

_____ o'clock

4. About how many cups of water will the jug hold?

○ 12
○ 28
○ 75

5. Emi saw 3 crows, 9 wrens, and 6 blue jays. How many birds did she see?

○ 12   ○ 15   ○ 18

Tuesday ⟨18⟩

1. $12 - 3 - 5 =$ _____

2. 23
      + 4
    ‾‾‾‾

3. Count by twos.

62 ___ ___ ___ ___

4. Draw an AABBAABB pattern.

5. Tory made a dozen cupcakes. Half of the cupcakes had chocolate frosting. How many cupcakes did not?

_____ cupcakes

Wednesday 〈18〉

1. 6 + 8 + 3 = _____

2. 17
  − 9
  _____

3. Which container holds just 4 cups of milk?

a.   b.   c.

4. Fill in the correct symbol.

$$< \ = \ >$$

8 + 7 ◯ 12 − 3

5. Connie saw 18 birds in a tree. Then 5 birds flew away. How many are still in the tree? How can you find the answer?

a. +   b. −   c. x

Thursday 〈18〉

1. 12 + 7 = _____

2. 18
  − 9
  _____

3. Are both sides the same?

yes   no

4. 11 ☐ 6 = 17

5. If the teacher asks each student to talk for 5 minutes about a hobby, how long would it take for 8 students to talk?

a. 13 minutes

b. 3 minutes

c. 40 minutes

Use these two shapes to make an ABBABBABB pattern.

Daily Math Practice

Daily Progress Record ⟨**18**⟩

How many did you get correct each day? Color the squares.

	Monday	Tuesday	Wednesday	Thursday	Friday
5					
4					
3					
2					
1					

Monday ⟨19⟩

1. $5 + 8 + 3 =$ _____

2. $\begin{array}{r} 12 \\ -5 \\ \hline \end{array}$

3. What comes next?

89 _____   75 _____

129 _____   111 _____

4. Count by tens.

120 _____   150 _____

190 _____

5. Marcus needs 18¢ for a pen. If he has 12¢, how much more does he need?

_____ ¢

Tuesday ⟨19⟩

1. $16 - 7 =$ _____

2. $\begin{array}{r} 5 \\ +9 \\ \hline \end{array}$

3. Mark $\frac{1}{2}$.

4. twenty – fourteen =

_____

5. Mrs. Reyes has worked at the store for 18 years. Mr. Lee has worked there for 9 years. How much longer has Mrs. Reyes worked at the store?

_____ years

1. $7 + 6 =$ _____

2. $\begin{array}{r} 17 \\ -\ 8 \\ \hline \end{array}$

3. Number in order from heavy to light.

____ ____ ____

4. $12 + 12 = 24$, so

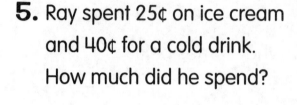

5. Ray spent 25¢ on ice cream and 40¢ for a cold drink. How much did he spend?

_____¢

1. $14 - 9 =$ _____

2. $\begin{array}{r} 46 \\ +\ 23 \\ \hline \end{array}$

3. Name the pattern.

_____

4. 3 is even.

　　　yes　　no

5. Ramon has stamps from many lands. He has 18 stamps from Mexico and 9 stamps from the USA. How many more Mexican stamps does he have?

_____ stamps

Begin at the star. Where is each object located?

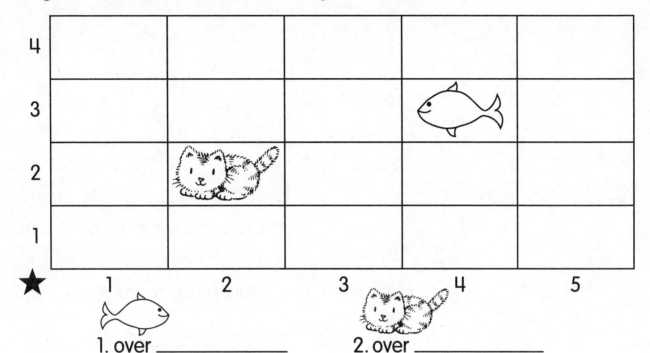

1. over _____

up _____

2. over _____

up _____

How many did you get correct each day? Color the squares.

	Monday	Tuesday	Wednesday	Thursday	Friday
5					▓
4					▓
3					▓
2					
1					

1. $17 - 9 =$ _____

2. $\begin{array}{r} 75 \\ + 14 \\ \hline \end{array}$

3. Count by twos.

88 ____   66 ____

44 ____

4. Fill in the correct symbol.

$$< \quad = \quad >$$

$$305 \bigcirc 159$$

5. There are 13 students in one class that walk to school and 5 students that ride the bus. How many more walk?

_____ students

---

1. $14 + 10 + 4 =$ _____

2. eleven – eight = _____

3. How long is the straw?

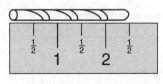

_____ inches

4. $12 + \boxed{} = 24$

5. Write four number sentences using 8, 9, and 17.

____ + ____ = ____

____ + ____ = ____

____ – ____ = ____

____ – ____ = ____

 EMC 6712 • © Evan-Moor Corp.

1. $14 - 7 - 3 =$ _____

2. $\begin{array}{r} 11 \\ + \ 8 \\ \hline \end{array}$

3. How far is it around this shape?

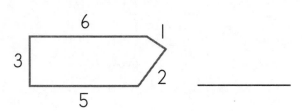

_____

4. Mark the odd numbers.

6   9   3   2

5. The salesman had 17 toy cars. He sold 3 green cars and 6 blue cars. How many did he have left?

_____ toy cars

1. $18 + 0 =$ _____

2. $\begin{array}{r} 15 \\ -13 \\ \hline \end{array}$

3. Write half past three on the clock.

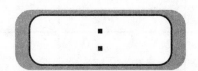

4. Color $\frac{1}{4}$.

5. There are saddles for half of the 18 horses in the barn. How many saddles are there?

_____ saddles

Friday ⟨20⟩

Mr. Lee's class is building bat houses. Each group of students needs a hammer, 10 nails, and 4 pieces of lumber.

If there are 5 groups, how many hammers, nails, and pieces of lumber will be needed?

_____ hammers   _____ nails

_____ pieces of lumber

Daily Progress Record ⟨20⟩

How many did you get correct each day? Color the squares.

	Monday	Tuesday	Wednesday	Thursday	Friday
5					▓
4					▓
3					
2					
1					

1. $13 - 8 =$ _____

2. $\begin{array}{r} 12 \\ +\ 12 \\ \hline \end{array}$

3. Make an **X** on the fourth candy cane.

4. Fill in the correct symbol.

< = >

eight ◯ six + two

5. Cody needs a new T-shirt. He has $15. If the T-shirt costs $12, how much change will he get back?

$_____

1. $16 - 9 =$ _____

2. $\begin{array}{r} 23 \\ +\ 15 \\ \hline \end{array}$

3. Write the numbers in order.

20 35 40 25 30

____ ____ ____ ____ ____

4. What time is it?

 7:15

◯ quarter to 7
◯ quarter past 7
◯ 7 o'clock

5. Marla bought six paper hats, six balloons, and six place mats. How many friends will be at her party?

_____ friends

1. $7 + 0 + 5 =$ _____

4. Fill in the correct symbol.

$$< \; = \; >$$

$10 + 8 \bigcirc 9 + 10$

2. $\begin{array}{r} 117 \\ -\ 17 \\ \hline \end{array}$

3. Name the pattern.

_____

5. Write four names for 13.

_____   _____

_____   _____

1. $13 + 10 =$ _____

4. How many dimes are in 80¢?

_____ dimes

2. $\begin{array}{r} 36 \\ -\ 12 \\ \hline \end{array}$

5. How many mittens are in nine pairs?

○ less than 10

○ more than 10

○ more than 20

3. ____ tens and ____ ones = ____

EMC 6712 • © Evan-Moor Corp.

Friday ⟨21⟩

How Many Fingers?

Use the finger picture to help.	
1 kid ___10___	6 kids _____
2 kids ___20___	7 kids _____
3 kids _____	8 kids _____
4 kids _____	9 kids _____
5 kids _____	10 kids _____

What pattern do you see?

_____

Daily Progress Record ⟨21⟩

How many did you get correct each day? Color the squares.

	Monday	Tuesday	Wednesday	Thursday	Friday
5					
4					
3					
2					
1					

1. $9 + 8 =$ _____

2. $\begin{array}{r} 219 \\ -106 \\ \hline \end{array}$

3. Write the numbers in order.

9   11   6   3   20

___ ___ ___ ___ ___

4. How many eggs are in a dozen?

12   18   10

5.

	1 hour ago	now	1 hour later
		3:15	
		7:45	
		11:30	

1. $19 - 9 =$ _____

2. $\begin{array}{r} 50¢ \\ +20¢ \\ \hline \end{array}$

3. Mark the sphere.

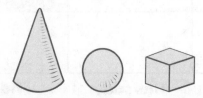

4. Draw a shape with 4 sides and 4 corners.

5. Dad cooked 15 hot dogs and 23 hamburgers for the picnic. How many pieces of meat did he cook in all?

a. 38   b. 56   c. 37

    EMC 6712 • © Evan-Moor Corp.

Wednesday ⟨22⟩

1. $18 - 6 - 3 =$ _____

2. $\begin{array}{r} 164 \\ + 230 \\ \hline \end{array}$

3. What time is it?

_____ : _____

4. $100 + 0 = 100$, so

$100 - \boxed{} = 100$

5. Julie spent 20¢, Joe spent 25¢, and Bill spent 32¢. How much did they spend altogether?

_____ ¢

Thursday ⟨22⟩

1. $9 + 6 + 3 =$ _____

2. $\begin{array}{r} 158 \\ - 114 \\ \hline \end{array}$

3. $6 + 9 = 15$, so

$9 + 6 = \boxed{}$

4. $12 \boxed{} 3 = 9$

5. Eight books were on the bottom shelf. Five books were on the second shelf. Four books were on the top shelf. How many books were there in all?

_____ books

Friday ⟨22⟩

How many squares can you count?

_____ squares

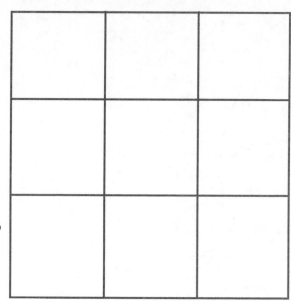

Daily Math Practice

Daily Progress Record ⟨22⟩

How many did you get correct each day? Color the squares.

	Monday	Tuesday	Wednesday	Thursday	Friday
5					
4					
3					
2					
1					

Monday 23

1. 27 − 16 = _____

2.   21
    +   7
   ———

3. Mark the even numbers.

    4   7   1   10

4. 20 − 10 = 10, so

    □ + 10 = 20

5. Inez needs 90¢ to buy a jar of paste. She has 50¢. How much more money does Inez need?

    _____¢

Tuesday 23

1. 13 + 5 = _____

2.   52
    + 26
   ———

3. Count by twos.

    100 102 _____ _____

    _____ _____

4. Write one hundred.

    _____

5. A spider has eight legs. If the spider wore shoes, how many pairs would it need?

    _____ pairs of shoes

1. $90 + 6 =$ _____

2.
$$\begin{array}{r} 14 \\ -3 \\ \hline \end{array}$$

3.
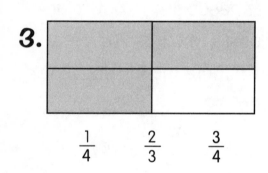

$\dfrac{1}{4}$ $\dfrac{2}{3}$ $\dfrac{3}{4}$

4. 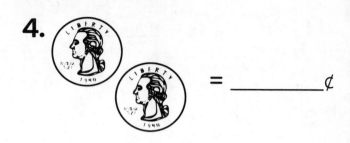 = _____ ¢

5. Yoshi saw frogs eating insects. One frog ate 7 insects, one ate 6, and another ate 5. How many insects did the frogs eat?

_____ insects

1. $60 - 20 =$ _____

2.
$$\begin{array}{r} 25 \\ +12 \\ \hline \end{array}$$

3. Fill in the correct symbol.

< = >

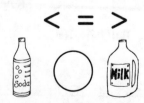

4. 8 tens and 7 ones is _____.

5. Mr. Garcia has a lot of animals. He has three dogs, six cats, two hamsters, and five birds. How many animals does he have?

_____ animals

Fill in the chart.

How many coins do you need?

9¢		1	4
11¢			
16¢			
24¢			

Daily Math Practice

Daily Progress Record 〈23〉

How many did you get correct each day? Color the squares.

	Monday	Tuesday	Wednesday	Thursday	Friday
5					
4					
3					
2					
1					

Monday 24

1. $26 - 5 =$ _____

4. $15 - 12 + 6 =$ _____

2.
$$\begin{array}{r} 12 \\ 15 \\ + 21 \\ \hline \end{array}$$

3. Count by tens.

_____ 140   _____ 110

_____ 200   _____ 180

5. The tall circus clown asked 6 children to feed the elephant 3 peanuts each. How many peanuts did the elephant eat?

○ 63   ○ 9   ○ 18

Tuesday 24

1. $26¢ + 15¢ =$ _____

4. Write nineteen.

_____

2.
$$\begin{array}{r} 20 \\ - 8 \\ \hline \end{array}$$

3.
$$\begin{array}{r} \text{nine} \\ \text{two} \\ \text{three} \\ + \text{ one} \\ \hline \end{array}$$

5. It is 2:00. It takes Johan 30 minutes to walk home from the park. What time will he get home?

70

1. $17 - 7 =$ _____

2. $\begin{array}{r} 416 \\ +\ 130 \\ \hline \end{array}$

3. How many sides?

_____

How many corners?

_____

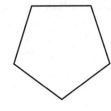

4. Fill in the correct symbol.

$< \ = \ >$

twelve ◯ two

5. How many hippos are there if 15 are on the riverbank and 7 are in the water?

_____ hippos

1. $18 - 6 - 3 =$ _____

2. $\begin{array}{r} 30 \\ 15 \\ +\ 21 \\ \hline \end{array}$

3. Draw an AABAAB pattern.

4.  $=$ _____

5. Today 29 monkeys escaped from the zoo. So far 16 have been caught. How many monkeys are still loose?

_____ monkeys

Paul has 40 marbles. Carmen has 10 more marbles than Paul. Albert has 10 more than Carmen.

How many marbles does Albert have?

_____ marbles

How many more marbles does Albert have than Paul?

_____ marbles

Daily Math Practice

Daily Progress Record ⟨**24**⟩

How many did you get correct each day? Color the squares.

	Monday	Tuesday	Wednesday	Thursday	Friday
5					▓
4					▓
3					▓
2					
1					

Monday ⬡25

1. 37 + 10 = _____

4. ☐ + 6 = 16

2.   218
      −   6

3. Write the numbers in order.

169 167 170 166 168

____ ____ ____ ____ ____

5. Glenn's grandfather is 56 years old. His brother is 12 years old. How much older is Glenn's grandfather?

_____ years

Tuesday ⬡25

1. 30 + 50 = _____

4. 1 hour = _____ minutes

2.   45
      − 14

3. Mark the words that tell how you can measure milk.

gallon   foot   liter
pound   quart   meter

5. Joan put 37¢ into her piggy bank. She took out 2 nickels and 3 pennies. How much money is left in Joan's bank?

_____ ¢

1. $16 - 2 - 8 =$ _____

2.　15
　　+ 16

3. How are these objects different?

○ different shape　○ different color

○ different size　　○ they are the same

4. Write zero.

_____

5. The picnic started at 3:15. It lasted for three hours. Show what time it ended.

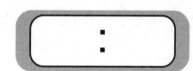

---

1. $16 - 11 =$ _____

2.　233
　　+ 420

3.

Which is first? _____

Which is last? _____

4. Make 32 tally marks.

5. Penny's pet hen laid an egg a day for two weeks. How many eggs did the hen lay?

_____ eggs

EMC 6712 • © Evan-Moor Corp.

Friday 〈25〉

Complete the chart. Write the letter of each object in the correct box.

SPHERE	CIRCLE

A   B   C

D   E   F

Now draw one more object in each box.

Daily Math Practice

Daily Progress Record 〈25〉

How many did you get correct each day? Color the squares.

	Monday	Tuesday	Wednesday	Thursday	Friday
5					
4					
3					
2					
1					

Monday 〈26〉

1. 25 – 15 = _____

2. 19
      + 9
     _____

3. Write an odd number.

_____

4. Fill in the correct symbol.

< = >

sixteen ◯ nineteen

5. If Willie has 23 chickens in a pen and 11 escape, how many chickens will still be in the pen?

_____ chickens

Tuesday 〈26〉

1. 24 + 43 = _____

2. 33
      – 16
     _____

3. What time is it?

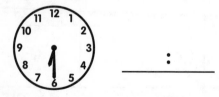

_____ :

4. 64 = ____ tens and ____ ones

5. There are 36 boys and 23 girls in second grade. How many more boys are there?

_____ more boys

1. $8 + 8 + 4 + 4 =$ _____

4. $30 - \boxed{} = 20$

2. $\begin{array}{r} 35 \\ -\ 0 \\ \hline \end{array}$

5. Write a word problem for $15 + 5.$

_____

_____

3. Count by fives.

75 ___ ___ ___ ___

_____

---

1. $15 + 10 + 14 =$ _____

4. $16 + 4 = 20,$ so

$20 - 4 = \boxed{}$

2. $\begin{array}{r} 68 \\ -28 \\ \hline \end{array}$

5. Maizie made 3 cakes. She put 7 candles on each cake. How many candles did she use?

3. Write the next numbers in the pattern.

$2 \quad 5 \quad 8 \quad 11$ ___ ___

○ 0   ○ 21   ○ 17

Draw an AABCAABC pattern.

Daily Math Practice

Daily Progress Record 〈**26**〉

How many did you get correct each day? Color the squares.

	Monday	Tuesday	Wednesday	Thursday	Friday
5					
4					
3					
2					
1					

EMC 6712 • © Evan-Moor Corp.

1. 20 + 60 + 10 = _____

2. 875
      – 452

3. Fill in the correct symbol.

< = >

216 ◯ 261

4. Match:

eighteen   20

thirteen   18

twenty   12

twelve   13

5. Herbert has 21 baseball cards. If he buys 13 more, how many cards will he have?

_____ cards

1. 5,893 + 0 = _____

2. 426
     + 231

3. Name the shape.

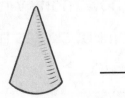 _____

4. Write an even number.

_____

5. Megan spent 35¢ on chips and 50¢ on a cold drink. How much did her snack cost?

_____¢

1. $6 + 12 + 10 =$ _____

2. $\begin{array}{r} 20 \\ -\ 8 \\ \hline \end{array}$

3. How much of this pie has been eaten?

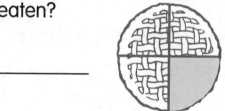

_____

4. 1 hundred + 2 tens + 0 ones =

_____

5. Max was paid 75¢ for walking Mrs. Lee's dogs. He gave Bob 35¢ for helping him. How much money did Max have left?

_____¢

1. $294 - 294 =$ _____

2. $\begin{array}{r} 53 \\ +28 \\ \hline \end{array}$

3. How long is the pencil?

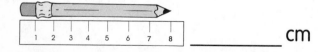

_____ cm

4. Which is the most money?
- ○ 4 dimes
- ○ 6 nickels
- ○ 2 quarters

5. If one pair of roller skates has 8 wheels, how many wheels will two pairs of skates have?

_____ wheels

Friday 〈27〉

Start with 1 dozen. _____

Take away the sides of a . − _____

Take away the number of legs on a goat. − _____

Add the corners on a . + _____

How many do you have? _____

Daily Math Practice

Daily Progress Record 〈27〉

How many did you get correct each day? Color the squares.

	Monday	Tuesday	Wednesday	Thursday	Friday
5					
4					
3					
2					
1					

1. 140 − 40 = _____

2. 15
     + 45
     ____

3. Write the numbers in order.

   290   300   280

   _____ _____ _____

4. Make an **X** on the oval shape.

5. Jeff's sled cost $45 and his ice skates cost $32. How much did Jeff spend?

   $_____

1. 31 + 11 + 22 = _____

2. 60
     − 27
     ____

3. Count by twos.

   _____ 118 _____

4. How heavy is the rock?
   ○ 8 feet
   ○ 8 inches
   ○ 8 ounces

5. Mother baked 3 dozen cookies. How many cookies did she bake?

   _____ cookies

1. 16 – 3 – 5 = _____

4. 24 + [　　] = 48

2. 64
　　+ 9
　　‾‾‾‾

5. Dennis bought a bag of jelly beans. There were 23 green, 41 red, and 15 black jelly beans. How many jelly beans were in the bag?

_____ jelly beans

3. What is the perimeter?

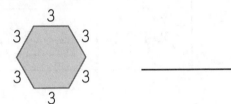

_____

1. 4,269 + 0 = _____

4. Write this time on the clock: 15 minutes after 3

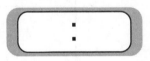

2. 29
　　– 15
　　‾‾‾‾

3. Complete the pattern.

3　6　9 ___ ___ ___

5. Jobeth and Martina each read 14 books last summer. How many books in all?

_____ books

Friday ⟨28⟩

Read the graph. Then answer the questions.

1. How many children wore shoes with:

Velcro® _____ buckles _____ shoelaces _____

2. What kind of shoe did most children wear?

_____

3. What kind of shoe did the fewest children wear?

_____

4. How many children are shown on the graph?

_____

Shoes	
= 2 children	
buckles	
shoelaces	
Velcro®	
pull-on	

Daily Progress Record ⟨28⟩

How many did you get correct each day? Color the squares.

	Monday	Tuesday	Wednesday	Thursday	Friday
5					
4					
3					
2					
1					

1. 16 − 4 − 5 = _____

2.

    37
  + 43

3. Mark the second letter.

R   B   X   J   Z   W

4. 182 =

_____ hundred _____ tens

_____ ones

5. For art class there are 12 each of blue, yellow, green, and red pencils. How many pencils are there in all?

_____ pencils

---

1. 4 + 4 + 4 + 4 = _____

2.
   542
 − 542

3. Count by tens.

100 _____   160 _____

130 _____

4. Fill in the correct symbol.

< = >

pound 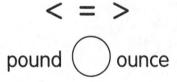 ounce

5. There were 49 geese swimming in the pond, and then 23 flew away. How many were left?

_____ geese

1. $65 + 12 =$ _____

4. $6 + 4 = 5 + \square$

2.
$$\begin{array}{r} 42 \\ -\ 36 \\ \hline \end{array}$$

5. Naomi wants an ice-cream cone with two scoops of ice cream. A scoop of ice cream is 30¢ and a cone is 25¢. How much will it cost?

_____¢

3. Color $\frac{1}{2}$.

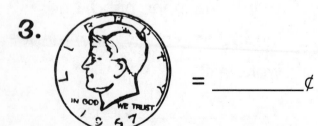

1. $99 - 28 =$ _____

4. $15 - \square = 9$

2.
$$\begin{array}{r} 223 \\ 104 \\ +\ 561 \\ \hline \end{array}$$

5. What is half of 20? _____

Tell how you got that answer.

_____

_____

_____

3. 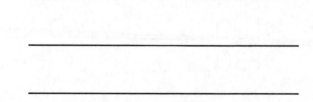 = _____¢

How many feet do these goats have? Use the goat picture to help you.

How Many Legs?	
1 goat __4__ legs	4 goats ____ legs
2 goats ____ legs	5 goats ____ legs
3 goats ____ legs	6 goats ____ legs

What pattern do you see?

_____

How many did you get correct each day? Color the squares.

	Monday	Tuesday	Wednesday	Thursday	Friday
5					
4					
3					
2					
1					

Monday 30

1. $16 + 15 =$ _____

2. $\begin{array}{r} 175 \\ -\ 41 \\ \hline \end{array}$

3. Write the numbers in order.

52 100 11 93 87

___ ___ ___ ___ ___

4. 5 is even.

yes   no

5. Sheree found 46 shells and James found 25 shells. How many shells did they find?

_____ shells

Tuesday 30

1. $17 - 12 =$ _____

2. $\begin{array}{r} 63 \\ +28 \\ \hline \end{array}$

3. If half an hour is 30 minutes, how long is an hour?

_____ minutes

4. $9 + 6 = 6 + \boxed{}$

5. The Blue Jays had 68 points. The Red Birds had 26 points. Which team won the game?

_____

By how many points did they win?

_____ points

Wednesday ⟨30⟩

1. 32 − 19 = _____

2. 14
     + 9
    ‾‾‾‾‾

3. Mark the numbers that tell about money.

 2¢ $5   5:00   10 cents   12 cm

4. 50 − 25 = 25, so

 ☐ + 25 = 50

5. A farmer has 4 pigs. Each pig has 6 piglets. How many piglets are there in all?

 _____ piglets

Thursday ⟨30⟩

1. 15 + 21 = _____

2. 32
     − 7
    ‾‾‾‾‾

3. Count by 5s.

 20 ____   35 ____

 50 ____   85 ____

4. Complete the pattern.

 18   16   14   ___   ___

5. The movie started at 2:00. It lasted for 2 and a half hours. At what time did the movie end?

 _____ : _____

Make the tally marks to show how many of each kind of flower.

6 _____ 3 _____

8 _____ 10 _____

Now color one space on the graph for each flower.

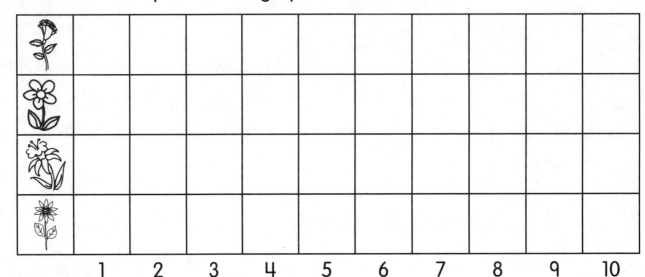

| | 1 | 2 | 3 | 4 | 5 | 6 | 7 | 8 | 9 | 10 |

Daily Math Practice

Daily Progress Record 30

How many did you get correct each day? Color the squares.

	Monday	Tuesday	Wednesday	Thursday	Friday
5					
4					
3					
2					
1					

1. 18 − 5 = _____

2.   35
      + 41
      ─────

3. Name the shape.

_____

4. Complete the pattern.

1   3   5   7   ____   ____   ____

5. Grandma bought a turkey. It cost $24. She gave the clerk $30. How much change did she get back?

$_____

1. 100 + 100 = _____

2.   60
      − 25
      ─────

3. Write the numbers in order.

58   52   50   54   56

____ ____ ____ ____ ____

4.

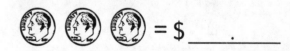 = $ _____ .

5. A fisherman caught 28 fish. He sold 18 fish and gave away 5 fish. How many did he have left?

_____ fish

Wednesday ⟨31⟩

1. $56 - 31 =$ _____

2.
$$
\begin{array}{r}
22 \\
34 \\
+\ 13 \\
\hline
\end{array}
$$

3. Draw a line of symmetry.

4. $16 - \boxed{} = 2$

5. Angela earns $2 every week. She has saved her money for 8 weeks to buy a soccer ball. How much money does she have?

$_____

Thursday ⟨31⟩

1. $13 + 48 =$ _____

2.
$$
\begin{array}{r}
50 \\
-\ 43 \\
\hline
\end{array}
$$

3. Color $\frac{2}{4}$.

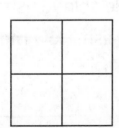

4. $4 \boxed{} 3 = 12$

5. Matt baked 20 cupcakes. He and his friends ate half of the cupcakes. How many are left?

_____ cupcakes

EMC 6712 • © Evan-Moor Corp.

Friday ⟨31⟩

Circle the two sets of shapes that can be used to make a hexagon.

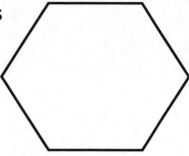

a. △ △ △ △ △

b. □ □ □

c. ▱ ▱

d. △ ▱

Daily Progress Record ⟨31⟩

How many did you get correct each day? Color the squares.

	Monday	Tuesday	Wednesday	Thursday	Friday
5					
4					
3					
2					
1					

1. $2 \times 2 =$ _____

2. 25
   $-$ 18

3. What comes next?

489 _____   730 _____

554 _____

4. Write the number word for 13.

_____

5. Last year Christopher weighed 48 pounds. This year he weighs 60 pounds. How much weight has he gained?

_____ pounds

---

1. $16 + 18 =$ _____

2. 94
   $-$ 27

3. What time is it?

_____ : _____

4. $15 + 15 = 30$, so

 $- 15 = 15$

5. Gina's father picked 12 oranges. He gave the same number of oranges to his four children. How many oranges did each one get?

_____ oranges

1. $15 - 8 - 7 =$ _____

2. $\begin{array}{r} 23 \\ + 21 \\ \hline \end{array}$

3. Fill in the correct symbol.

$$< \ = \ >$$

$100¢\ \bigcirc\ \$1$

4. Circle the number that is the most likely to be picked without looking.

| 6 | 3 | 4 |
| 3 | 1 | 3 | 6 |

1   3   4   6

5. A quart of milk is equal to 4 cups. Mother used 3 quarts to make ice cream for the picnic. How many cups of milk did she use?

_____ cups

1. $4 \times 2 =$ _____

2. $\begin{array}{r} 61 \\ - 34 \\ \hline \end{array}$

3. Complete the pattern.

15 12 9 ___ ___

4. This is a sphere.

yes   no

5. Jose opened his piggy bank. He found 2 quarters, 3 dimes, and 17 pennies. How much money did he have?

_____¢

Divide the cookies into 3 equal groups.

_____ in each group

Daily Math Practice

Daily Progress Record ⟨32⟩

How many did you get correct each day? Color the squares.

	Monday	Tuesday	Wednesday	Thursday	Friday
5					
4					
3					
2					
1					

1. 46 − 32 = _____

2.
$$810 \atop + \ 76$$

3. Show how 4 kids can share.

4. Write the numbers in order.

442 408 473 459

_____ _____ _____ _____

5. The bakery sold 31 pies on Sunday, 22 pies on Monday, and 16 pies on Tuesday. How many pies were sold in three days?

_____ pies

1. 5 × 2 = _____

2.
$$95 \atop -38$$

3. Circle the names for 8.

4 + 4   16 − 8

12 − 5   4 × 2

4. Show 15 minutes after 5 on the clock.

5. If there are 8 legs on one spider, how many legs are on 5 spiders?

_____ legs

1. 76 − 30 = _____

2. 53
   + 37

3. Which shape does NOT belong?

a.

b. ▢

c.

d.

4. Mark the ninth dot.

5. Write four number sentences using 6, 12, and 18.

____ + ____ = ____

____ + ____ = ____

____ − ____ = ____

____ − ____ = ____

1. 29 − 7 = _____

2. 2
   × 3

3. These shapes are congruent. Why?   ▢ ▢

○ same size, different shape

○ same size, same shape

○ different size, same shape

○ different size, different shape

4. 406 =

____ hundreds   ____ tens

____ ones

5. Jerome spent 20 minutes on his spelling and 15 minutes reading a book. Did he work longer than a half hour?

yes   no

How much does your name cost?

a e i o u	g j p q y	all other letters
$ .50	$1.00	$ .25

Sal

$ .25
   .50
+ .25
─────
$

Your Name

Daily Math Practice

Daily Progress Record 〈33〉

How many did you get correct each day? Color the squares.

	Monday	Tuesday	Wednesday	Thursday	Friday
5					
4					
3					
2					
1					

1. $3 \times 3 =$ _____

2. $\begin{array}{r} 20 \\ + 70 \\ \hline \end{array}$

3. Write the numbers in order.

90 85 75 95 80

___ ___ ___ ___ ___

4. Fill in the correct symbol.

$< \; = \; >$

fifteen ◯ two + four

5. There are 23 grasshoppers, 106 ladybugs, and 210 ants in the backyard. How many insects are there?

_____ insects

1. $31 + 18 =$ _____

2. $\begin{array}{r} 62 \\ - 19 \\ \hline \end{array}$

3. Draw a shape with 5 sides and 5 corners.

4. $4 \times \boxed{} = 12$

5. Write a word problem for $16 - 14$.

_____

_____

_____

1. $5 \times 5 =$ _____

4. $15 + 24 = 24 +$ ☐

2.   133
     + 126

5. A group of 48 campers went on a hike. Soon 4 hikers got tired and stopped. Then 3 hikers got sick and stopped. How many campers made it to the end of the hike?

_____ campers

3. Fill in the correct symbol.

< = >

1. $66 - 32 =$ _____

4. $3 \times$ ☐ $= 9$

2.   34
     + 49

5. The party started at 3:00. It ended at 5:30 in the afternoon. How long did the party last?

_____ hours

3. How long is the key?

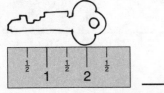

_____ inches

Friday ⬡ 34

How many coins do you need?

28¢	I			3
35¢				
49¢				

Daily Progress Record ⬡ 34

How many did you get correct each day? Color the squares.

	Monday	Tuesday	Wednesday	Thursday	Friday
5					
4					
3					
2					
1					

1. $2 \times 3 =$ _____

2. $\begin{array}{r} 87 \\ + 13 \\ \hline \end{array}$

3. Divide the squares in half 4 different ways.

4. $25 \ \boxed{} \ 10 = 15$

5. Today 253 students are eating a hot lunch and 106 brought lunch from home. How many students are eating lunch at school?

_____ students

1. $10 + 24 + 42 =$ _____

2. $\begin{array}{r} 62 \\ - 27 \\ \hline \end{array}$

3. Count by tens.

140 _____ _____

_____ _____

4. $13 + 12 = 25$, so

$25 - \boxed{} = 12$

5. It costs Sarah $10.77 a week to feed her pets. If she spends $6.52 on her dog, how much does she spend on her cat?

$_____

1. $2 \times 4 =$ _____

2.   473
       + 304
       _____

3. Mark the clock that shows a quarter past 9.

4. Fill in the correct symbol.

$$< \ = \ >$$

$0 \times 5 \bigcirc 9 \times 0$

5. It is 469 miles to Uncle Ted's house. How far did Austin and Jordan travel today if they have 143 miles left to go?

_____ miles

---

1. $64 + 16 =$ _____

2.   629
       − 416
       _____

3. $6 \div 2 =$ _____

4. Draw a shape with no corners.

5. Brian bought a pencil for 25¢. He paid for it with a half dollar. How much change did he get back?

a. 14¢   b. 50¢   c. 25¢

Friday 35

If I take one cookie without looking, what is the chance I'll get each of these cookies?

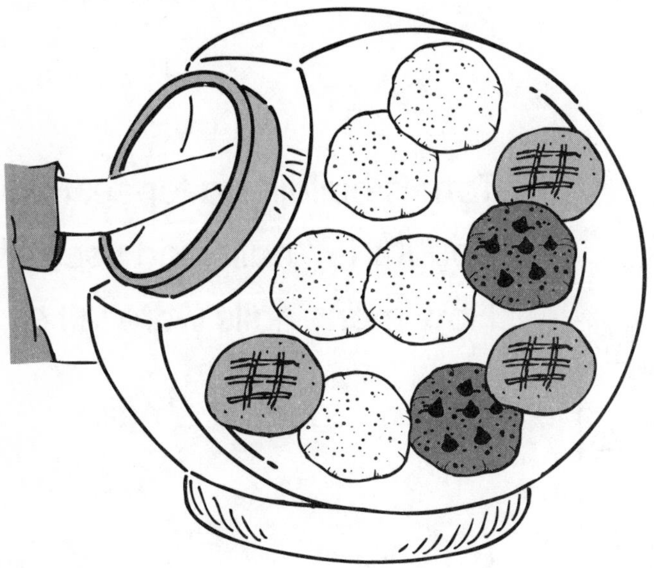

1. 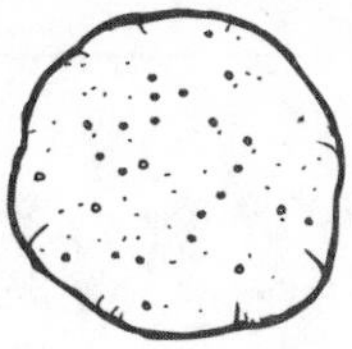 sugar cookie	Most likely Least likely Impossible
2. 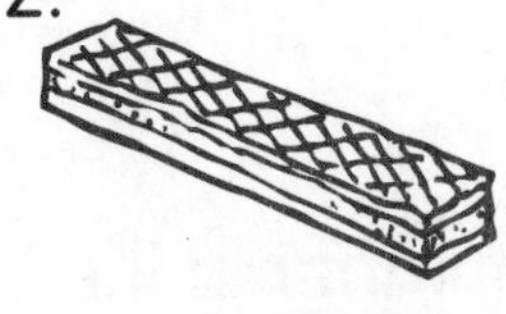 sugar wafer	Most likely Least likely Impossible
3. 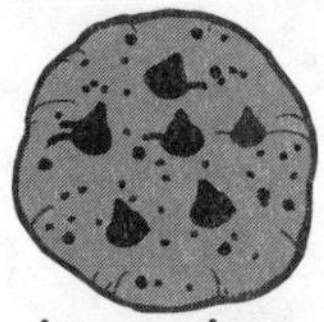 chocolate cookie	Most likely Least likely Impossible

Daily Math Practice

Daily Progress Record 35

How many did you get correct each day? Color the squares.

	Monday	Tuesday	Wednesday	Thursday	Friday
5					
4					
3					
2					
1					

Monday 36

1. $24 - 17 =$ _____

2. $28 + 35 =$ _____

3. Write each number in the correct box.

1 9 2 8 3 4 10 5 7 6

Even	Odd

4. $35 + 20 = 55$, so

$55 -$ ☐ $= 35$

5. Tom is building a tepee. He bought 167 nails and used 94. How many nails were left?

_____ nails

Tuesday 36

1. $3 \times 4 =$ _____

2.
$$
\begin{array}{r}
14 \\
64 \\
+ 23 \\
\hline
\end{array}
$$

3. How many sides does a cube have?

_____ sides

4. Fill in the correct symbol.

< = >

$900 \bigcirc 899$

5. A new bike costs $137. Carolina has saved $84. How much more does she need?

$ _____

1. 40 + 18 = _____

2. 50
   − 22

3. What time will it be in 30 minutes?

  a. 4:00 c. 4:15
  b. 4:30 d. 4:45

4. Estimate.

    250 + 375 =
  a. 600 b. 125 c. 5,000

5. After the soccer game, the team went to Kelly's house. They ate 27 cookies and 16 brownies. How many snacks did the team eat?

_____ snacks

1. 3 × 5 = _____

2. 123
  + 635

3. How long is the ribbon?

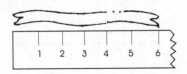

_____ cm

4. 10 ÷ 2 = _____

5. Last Saturday, 128 adults and 164 children went to the ball game. How many people were at the game?

_____ people

Friday 36

Tomas ate $\frac{1}{2}$ of the jelly beans. Lisa ate $\frac{1}{4}$ of the jelly beans. If there were 20 jelly beans, how many did they eat?

Tomas _____   Lisa _____

How many jelly beans were left?

_____ jelly beans

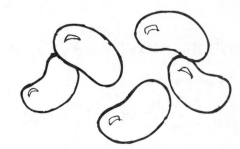

Daily Math Practice

Daily Progress Record 36

How many did you get correct each day? Color the squares.

	Monday	Tuesday	Wednesday	Thursday	Friday
5					▓
4					▓
3					▓
2					
1					

How to Solve
Word Problems

 Read the problem carefully. Think about what it says.

 Look for clue words. The clue words will tell you if you should add or subtract.

 Solve the problem.

 Check your work. Make sure your answer makes sense.

Clue Words

Add	Subtract
in all	more than
altogether	less than
total	are left
sum	take away
both	difference
plus	fewer

112